To See a World in a Grain of Sand

Poems by Art Elser

Copyright © 2018 Art Elser
All rights reserved.

No part of this book may be reproduced or transmitted in any form or by any means, electronic or mechanical, including photocopying, recording, or by any information storage and retrieval system without the expressed written permission of the author, except in the case of brief quotations in critical articles and reviews.

ISBN-978-0-9984554-4-0

WalkerDoodle Press
Denver, CO 80220

As always to Kate —
my inspiration
and love of my life

Acknowledgements

These journals have previously published the poems listed, some in slightly different versions:

Emerging Voices: A Glacial Erratic, After the Martin Luther King Parade, Did the hand then of the potter shake?, Dinner of Fire and Ice, Morning Thoughts Over Coffee, Requiem for a Gay Young Man, The Edges of Humanity.

High Plains Register: Death on a City Sidewalk, Descending Into Puerto Vallarta, Left Behind By Its Nomad Tribe, Morning at the VLA Radio Telescope, Out of Step.

Labyrinth: A Siren Keens in the Darkness.

Open Window Review: Flying Horse of Gansu, Surprised by Joy, The Old Picture in the Back Hall.

Owen Wister Review: Introspective Light, Late Spring Storm.

Passager: October 24, 1962, 3:45 AM.

Proud To Be: My Band of Brothers, The Church Ruins at Quang Ngai.

Science Poetry: Sunspots Explained.

Serendipity Poets Journal: A Murder of Crows.

The Human Touch: A Villanelle of War, I read to My New Grandson, In the Doctor's Waiting Room, The Sudden End of the Firefight. To See a World in a Grain of Sand.

The Weekly Avocet: Long Ago Snows, Ridge Soaring in Virginia, Song of the Earth—song sung blue.

Vietnam War Poetry: Book of Names.

To see a world in a grain of sand,
And a heaven in a wild flower,
Hold infinity in the palm of your hand,
And eternity in an hour.

William Blake "Auguries of Innocence"

Contents

Acknowledgements v

Blueberry Summers 3
Blueberry Summers 5
I Meet Ceola 6
An Old Photo Stirs a Memory 8
The Passing of Innocence 10
I Read to My New Grandson 11
Today I Listen to Beethoven's Sixth 12
Long Ago Snows 13
Tara's Call of the Wild 14
Elegy for a Bricklayer 16
The Last Leaf to Fall 18
Flying Horse of Gansu 19
Late Spring Storm 20

Did the Hand Then of the Potter Shake? 21
"Did the Hand Then of the Potter Shake?" 23
If the Seed Knew 24
The Edges of Humanity 25
Busy Morning on a City Street Corner 26
Out of Step 27
Left Behind by Its Nomad Tribe 28
After the Martin Luther King Parade 29
Requiem for a Young Gay Man 30
Death on a City Sidewalk 31
Woman on Unsigned Acrylic 32
Da Vinci in a Denver Coffee Shop 33
In the Doctor's Waiting Room 34
Dinner of Fire and Ice 36
A Siren Keens in the Darkness 37
Il Carnevale di Venezia 38

Morning Thoughts Over Coffee 39
Introspective Light 41
Morning Thoughts Over Coffee 42
Morning at the VLA Radio Telescope 44

Rock, Paper, Scissors...45
Song of Earth – song sung blue..46
Surprised by Joy...47
High Plains Thunderstorm 48
Ridge Soaring in Virginia...50
A Murder of Crows...51
After the Summer Solstice..52
Ode to a Fairy Primrose...53
To See a World in a Grain of Sand..54

Sunspots Explained 55
  A Villanelle of War..57
  Sunspots Explained 58
  Hiroshima, August 6, 1945, 8:15 AM.....................................60
  October 24, 1962, 3:45 AM...61
  A Glacial Erratic...62
  Darkness at the Bottom of the Fog 64
  The Sudden End of the Firefight...65
  I Will Fight No More Forever..66
  The Old Picture in the Back Hall..67
  War Memorial at Holy Ghost Church....................................68
  The Church Ruins at Quang Ngai..69
  Descending into Puerto Vallarta..70
  Book of Names 71
  My Band of Brothers...72

About the Author 73

Blueberry Summers

Blueberry Summers

Five kids follow Aunt Vi along
a deeply worn path in the forest.
We each have a sack lunch, a pail,
a small pot to gather berries in.
A half mile later we cross an oiled
county road and walk a few yards
into the woods to a clearing with
hundreds of blueberry bushes.

At first we walk from bush to bush
but tire quickly and soon sit to pick.
One for the pot, for me, for the pot,
two for me . . . . Dump pot into pail,
start filling it again, eating some
as we move on to the next bush.

The berries are sun-warm and sweet
and leave dark blue stains on mouths
and hands that are tough to wash off.

I wash away the stains from picking
and eating those blueberries but not
the memories of blueberry summers.

I Meet Ceola

The other day I met Ceola.
I shook hands with her.
Her hands were rough, but gentle.
I never saw a person whose skin
is black like hers. None of the kids
in our school have black skin.
Black skin and a bright red bandana,
and when she smiles, her teeth and eyes
are so white. I like Ceola. She is very
gentle, like Aunt Vi.

I asked Aunt Vi about Ceola.
She said Ceola has grown children,
a daughter in Harlem and a son
fighting the Nazis in Italy.
She has a husband, Alfred.
They moved to New York from Georgia.
They live on a farm miles from any other house.
They plow their field with a mule.
They raise their own food.
They have a cow for milk.
They have no electricity.
Ceola comes to town once or twice
a month, sometimes on the mule,
to get kerosene and food they can't
grow on their farm.

I asked Mommy about Ceola.
She said Ceola has grown up children
who live somewhere else. I asked if I
could walk to Ceola's house
because she invited me.

Mommy got mad and said, "No!
Don't ever ask again!" When I asked
why Ceola smelled like kerosene,
she said, "All niggers smell like that.
Dogs smell like dogs, cows like cows,
and niggers like niggers."
I don't know why Mommy
got so mad.

I asked Daddy about Ceola.
He said, "Ceola is a good nigger
because she knows her place."
That was a funny answer.
Sure she knows her place.
Her place is her farm. And
she walks to town and back
a couple of times every month.
I don't know why Daddy
is so confused.

An Old Photo Stirs a Memory

My son and I head up the wide sandy trail
into Stanley Canyon. The smell of dust
kicked up by our boots mixes with the hot scent
of ponderosa pine. The trail gets steeper,
rockier, more difficult. We slow the pace.
A raven floats off a branch, circles, croaks.

We wind through the canyon and soon hear
a creek splashing as it descends the steep slope.
A mile and a half in, the splashing becomes a roar.
The air cools. We feel mist, smell hot pine pitch,
come to a waterfall. Spring's been wet so it drops
full, fast, furious.

We stop for lunch and, perched on warm rocks,
eat peanut butter and jelly sandwiches.
My son is antsy, gobbles his lunch, and scrambles
over large rocks twenty feet up to the waterfall's lip.
I snap a photo to show his mother. He climbs down
and we continue hiking up the canyon.

Soon the trail flattens, the creek slows.
We enter a quiet meadow with stands of aspen
and Gambel oak. I tell my son the names
of wildflowers —columbine, fireweed, sego lily.
The air is pungent with the rot of leaf-fall.

At the top we hear the rumble of nearby thunder.
The sky darkens. We hurry to set up the tent,
barely get the fly staked when the storm hits.

First heavy rain, then hail. We crawl into the tent,
unroll sleeping bags, stretch out on them, and nap,
lulled by hail drumming on the fly.

Later we fish in the reservoir for an hour,
catch nothing, but treasure the day.

The Passing of Innocence

A chance reading of a poem this morning
brought back a memory of my son,
singing in a middle school musical.
His was a minor part, but he sang it well,
his voice pure and clear and high.

Back then during the long drives home
at night from visiting family, we sang
to a tape of the Nylons, a group with one
male voice that reached falsetto highs.
My son would sing up there with him.

One night we sang along as always,
and at the point where we had to quit
and our son would sing up the ladder
of notes, his voice faltered. We knew
the age of his innocence was passing.

I Read to My New Grandson

>*May 22, 1995*

Softly, so I don't disturb others,
I read *Jonathan Livingston Seagull*
to you by the faint green lights
that trace your infant struggle
to live.

Your mother lies sleepless
in another room, weak
from birthing you today.
She sees only darkness.
But these dim lights assure me
you still live.

Reading to you of grace and courage,
I want you to hear
and use these words: friendship,
compassion, love, words that
I too need.

I touch you, to steady my fear,
as the green lights,
the color of hope and spring,
illuminate the words I read
to let you know you are not
alone.

Today I Listen to Beethoven's Sixth

and remember when you were three.
You lived with us and we loved it.
Thursday nights your Mamma and Nonna
would go to class, leaving us to ourselves.
We'd go to that Italian place you loved,
and you'd munch your way through
half a loaf of Italian bread while you
waited for your calamari to arrive.
Who ever heard of a three year old loving
calamari? But you'd eat a huge plate full.

We'd come home pleasantly stuffed —
laugh at Wily Coyote's cartoon pratfalls
until it was time for me to put you to bed.
Then I'd load Fantasia. We'd sit on the floor —
you on my lap — and wave our arms
to help Leopold Stokowski conduct.
Beethoven's Sixth Symphony played
and mythical fauns, cupids, and centaurs
danced in a wild world of color. I'd put
the music on hold as I stopped the tape,
move you to your bed, and restart it.
You'd off to sleep to the magic of Disney.

You're now half way through high school
and your tastes have undoubtedly changed.
When you hear Beethoven's Sixth Symphony
do you remember those long-ago evenings?
Are those memories today special to you?

Long Ago Snows

The muted silence of a foot of new snow
brings memories of a country road,
trackless in the morning, and our joyful
frolicking off to school with wool pants
tucked into galoshes, buckles fastened
to keep out the snow. The only sounds
are the shushing of boots and my sister's
laughter as she follows in the trail
I've broken. Then a car appears magically
behind us, tire chains clinking. A neighbor
slows to wait for us to move off the road
and waves as his car hums past. We rest
by walking in the tire tracks he makes,
heads wreathed in our breath, bodies
warmed by trudging, sliding, laughing.

Now, a lifetime later, the thought
of mushing those miles makes
me shiver. I no longer burn
with youthful heat. I hibernate
in the house and listen to
those long ago snows.

Tara's Call of the Wild

I lift our husky onto the vet's table,
careful not to put pressure on her
arthritic hips. she lays quietly as if
knowing what's about to happen.
I speak softly, hand on her flank.
The vet holds the needle, searches
for a vein and slides it in. He looks
at me and I nod. A few shallow
breaths and then a long, last exhale.
I cry as I feel her go still, something
she never does on our morning runs.

Tara pulls hard on the leash
to get me to run faster to the spot
where I slip off the leash to let her
run freely. She runs through meadows
finding things to investigate, coyotes
to play with, Hereford bulls to chase
away to protect me.

She often doesn't come when I
call her to slip the leash back on.
She gives me her Mona Lisa smile
and runs off to spend the next three
or four days visiting ranches.
A call. Tara is at their ranch.
She smiles as I put her in the car,
happy with her days of freedom.

When I feel her relax, her last breath
gone, I know her wild animal spirit
is now free to roam meadows, forever
smiling, running, chasing, never
coming to my call to go back home.

Elegy for a Bricklayer

I sat on my haunches as a child
and watched as you set
the pegs for the chalk lines,
chalked, and snapped them,

leaving a straight cerulean line
in the dirt. You mixed the sand,
cement, water to perfect consistency
so that a flick of your wrist

delivered mortar to the right spot
to accept the next brick.
It would lie level with the row
below it, the spacing exact

between it and the previous one.
You would then tap tap tap it
with the butt of the trowel until
it was perfectly fitted in place,

then scrape off excess mortar.
I watched you build wall after wall,
each one inside the blue lines
so they were level and square.

You talked about being careful, exact,
skillful in your work and in life.
You kept your life within those walls,
walls that contained certainty of thought,

black and white views of others, of how
they lived and behaved. So guarded
that you even walled out your family,
children, grandchildren.

When Mom died we had to add brick
steps to get into the front door.
You built walls with no flaws, but also
no entrance for humanity or love.

The Last Leaf to Fall

The shadows of desiccated leaves,
hanging from winter-bare branches,
fluttered on the hospital floor
the day my mother died.

She was the last of her generation,
outlived the rest by a dozen years.
She often said "I want to be with Dad."
Her last days were painful, hellish,
spine curled, head bent to her knees.
She was surrounded by other shriveled
women and men, who, like the leaves,
were barely hanging on.

Perhaps she waited for us to visit her
one last time. We held her hands
all morning, begging her to let go.
She did, but only after we left.
The same way a leaf will let go
when no one is watching it.

Flying Horse of Gansu

She brought the green bronze sculpture
from China forty years ago. It's one third
the size of the original. The horse exudes
the power and speed, grace and beauty
that the horse symbolized for the Chinese.
It balances perfectly with its right hind hoof
on the back of a startled swallow, the bird
itself a symbol of light and graceful flight.

Did she know when she first saw the horse
and loved it that she undoubtedly loved it
because it has the same dignity as her life?
Did she know when she gave it to me
at her death that I would always think
of her when I look at and love the horse?

Late Spring Storm

A gust of wind brings
rain and chill. We hurry
to bring in the food.
But then I see you on the chaise lounge,
blankets pulled to your chin,
eyes smiling, alive to the anarchy
of the evening storm.

Before, you would curse—
under your breath of course—
the storms that set
your outdoor dinner plans
on their head.

But in that summer of your dying
you discovered that life
has no guarantees,
and *that* had set you free.

Did the Hand Then of the Potter Shake?

"Did the Hand Then of the Potter Shake?"

Rubaiyat of Omar Khayyam

The young man, in his twenties, body bent
from years of pain, sails across a sea
of blacktop, his crutches, outriggers, held out
to steady him. But the storm of his affliction
overpowers the ineffectual rudder. He veers
off course, runs aground on an unseen bar,
and founders.

He fights to regain control,
to steer a safe passage.
But the relentless storm
blows him further
from shelter.
He is helpless
and defeated.

Why did the master shipwright
make him an unseaworthy vessel?
Is this a test for the young man?

Or does the shipwright simply
not care?

If the Seed Knew . . .

If the seed knew, would it drink
the rain, soak up the warmth
of the ever northward spring sun?

Would it so eagerly thrust the green
blade through the frosty ground
to chance a quick frozen death?

If it knew the petals of its flowers
would shrivel and fall to rot would
it push so hard to follow its DNA?

If he knew, would man be born,
fight through the birth canal,
struggle for that first breath?

If he knew that famine, disease,
hatred, bigotry, waited for him
would he fight so hard to be born?

If he knew those he loved would die
and his mind would sputter and fail,
would he still choose to be born?

The Edges of Humanity

Five derelicts, cast-offs
of humanity, huddle
near a fire in a barrel
in the corner of an alley,
tumbleweeds blown there
with the plastic bags and rags
of their lives. They are snagged
on the barbed wire of fate,
fear, alcohol, psychosis,
by choices made years before
with little thought of where
they might lead.

They laugh as they share
a meal and stories
and a brown paper sack
that each drinks from
before passing it on.
A stray dog cowers
from man to man.
They talk to it,
hug its neck,
scratch its ears,
and share a bit
of their meager meal.

Busy Morning on a City Street Corner

From a coffee shop I watch a disheveled man
in a stained blue jacket, hunched in a wheelchair,
as if life has pinned him there with its G forces.

His dirt stained hand waves a grimy plastic cup
with *Anything Helps* taped to it at people passing.
He scowls at those who don't drop something in.

His right hand often reaches into a torn canvas
bag to pull out a bottle wrapped in a paper bag.
After half an hour and several furtive swigs,
he eases the wheelchair to the curb and waits.

When the light changes he turns the wheelchair
and starts backwards across four lanes of traffic.
Half-hearted shoves of a single foot propel him.

The other foot drags on the pavement, hands
in his lap, not pushing. He halts and glares back
at drivers he delays when the light turns green.

He moves in fits and spurts along the sidewalk,
not looking where he's going; people dodge him.

He looks only to his past in tow behind him.

Out of Step

She shuffles through the crowd
in tattered boots, past tasseled loafers,
elegant pumps, and shiny wingtips
that dance-step warily around her.

Neat business suits and tailored skirts
avoid her soiled and tattered coat,
a drab-green rock creating an eddy
in a river of hurrying humanity.

Eyes that once must have smiled
at children and butterflies and sunsets,
peer numbly into the stream, searching
for hope she's certain isn't there.

Left Behind by Its Nomad Tribe

from Tom Hennen

I once saw a butterfly in November,
a flutter in a meadow of fall-dead grass.
Yellow wings flitting from stalk to stalk,
searching for a flower or small bit of nectar.
The sky that morning spoke of storm.
The butterfly would surely die, its yellow,
flashing wings interred in snow.

One spring I often saw a pronghorn doe
who limped around on an injured leg.
Most times, the bigger herd was not in sight.
At other times she'd hover near some does,
who slowly moved away, left her behind.
She surely could not run with the herd
when winter-hungry coyotes came.
And they would take her down and rip
and tear apart her still warm form.

Today I watched a rumpled man
limp down the street. His tattered coat,
that once had fit, now was loose.
His baggy pants were stained and torn
and hid his bone-thin form. His eyes
were dead, no spark, no life, no hope.
He's left behind by his nomad tribe.
He likely too will die alone.

After the Martin Luther King Parade

The old man scuttles across the grass,
below the gold-leafed capitol dome,
half running, half hopping, like a magpie.
A battered black coat shields him
from the January cold, and wind
feathers his white hair as he claws
through trash left by those
who watched the parade,
shoving bits of half-eaten
lunches into his maw.

A woman in a cashmere coat,
glances sidelong at him,
as she circles warily past.
And a man in a dark business suit
passes and shakes his head.

The old man continues to fly
from pile to pile of garbage,
eating and stuffing soda cans
into a sack, ignoring those
passing by.

Did *he* ever have a dream?

Requiem for a Young Gay Man

The young man, in black pants and coat,
white shirt, stands slumped at the window.
His pinched mouth works silently.
Absentmindedly, he strokes his short
black beard and stares
into the darkness at his feet.

After a long while, he moves to a small desk
and writes a note about the painful death
of his friend, of the virus they share —
the doctors doubt he'll live two more years -
of his father's angry, homophobic curse ...

Taking off his coat, he folds it, places it on the desk,
and sits cross-legged on the floor.
He rolls up a sleeve and leans lightly
against the wall. In the darkness he cannot see
the vein, but he's done this before and does it by feel.

The drugs course warmly through his blood.

He smiles beatifically. Then darkness
dims his eyes.

Death on a City Sidewalk

Frayed brown twine snakes
from a hand, visible beneath
a greasy blanket, across a crack
in the sidewalk to a faded
and torn tan valise.

Dirt-stained fingers,
knuckles bruised and cracked,
clutch the twine tied
to meager possessions.

A paramedic gently
pries the tattered twine
from the stiff hand,
leaving the valise
on the sidewalk
as the body is lifted
into an ambulance.

Other, eager, dirt-stained fingers,
snatch up the valise and clumsily
wrap the twine around the prize.

Woman on Unsigned Acrylic

A plain young woman beneath
a gloomy sky, defeat on her face,
turns to look over her shoulder

at the life she's decided to leave.
The blush on her cheeks almost
covers the bruises, but the pain

shows in her eyes and thin lips.
She's not taken the time to brush
unruly hair, just pulled it back

from her face, held it with a clip.
She does not cry, but her green
eyes say tears will soon come.

Trapped forever in that painting,
she looks backward in despair,
no hope or love or joy forever.

Da Vinci in a Denver Coffee Shop

An attractive young woman, mid 20s,
sits by herself at a small, round table.
Her blonde hair short and well groomed.
Her white t-shirt rolled at the shoulders.

Cell phone and brown leather wallet
beside her cup of black coffee.
Blue-gray eyes stare wistfully into space,
lips ever so slightly pursed.

Does she think about a love that's gone,
a missed opportunity, a risk not taken?
Does she wonder about the future,
career, love, children, sadness, joy?

A coffee shop Mona Lisa.

In the Doctor's Waiting Room

A short, dark-haired woman in her late sixties, in a red jacket,
leads her husband in and settles him in a chair.
She chats briefly with the receptionist,
her small hands flitting.
She sits down ninety degrees to her husband, watching over
 him.
They settle quietly, his long, thin white cane held at the ready
in his fleshy left hand.
His right hand rests on his knee and moves nervously
as if finding a message there in braille.

Another couple, also short and stocky, twenty years younger,
appears. The man whispers to the red jacket and sits.
He takes a car magazine offered by his wife.
She reads a medical magazine.
He unzips his leather jacket,
flips through pages,
scarcely looking at the pictures,
hunching over until his jacket resembles
the shell of a turtle.

His wife nervously scans her magazine, until she finds
 something,
and whispers urgently to him.
He pulls away and waves a pudgy hand at her with a short flick
of the wrist to stop her whispering.
She reads anyway,
symptoms of Parkinson's Disease.
Prognosis—no cure.
Treatment—none that lasts.

A nurse calls the older couple,
they rise, joined by their son.
The young wife fidgets,
sure she already knows what they are about to learn.

Dinner of Fire and Ice

She sits alone, eyes burning darkly.
Ten, twenty minutes. He finally comes,
hang dog, tail tucked between his legs.

He sits across the table, facing her.
Then I watch him move his chair
closer, reach to hold her hand.

He seems not to find words to explain
some deed that he has done to fire
her cold and hardly veiled contempt.

He finally speaks.
She nods curtly.
Not speaking.

Not looking at him.
They share wine.
It must taste bitter.

I finish dinner first, although I think
he was finished long before the wine.

A Siren Keens in the Darkness

finally winding down to silence. A wife,
a widow, although she does not yet know
she is, meets the ambulance and hurries
the medics through the rectangle of light
to her husband, slumped on the love seat.

Terrified, she watches as they minister
to him, nod gravely to her, then lift him
to the gurney, and cover his face.

The ambulance leaves silently . . .
the widow slumps to the floor . . .
the keening now hers in the darkness.

Il Carnevale di Venezia

Two paintings look out across the bedroom
from their gilded frames. Man and woman
in front of dark backgrounds, mysterious,

masked, somewhat foreboding. She wears
a gold gown covered by a black *mantilla*
and flowing black cape. One long, bare arm

rests languidly on the chair while the other
holds a black mask to her pale face. He wears
a black coat and ethereal, lacy white gloves.

His face is covered by a white leather mask,
a *bauta*. Half the mask is in light, the other
in shadow. *Il Carnevale* begins after Christmas

and closes at the start of Lent. From a period
of celebration to one of penance. Is the couple
evil, signified by the darkness they hide in?

Or do they move away from evil into the light?

Morning Thoughts Over Coffee

Introspective Light

The low, slant light of dawn
gives form to a hill and the ridge
that rides behind it.
Trees, startled from sleep, stand,
propped there by shadows.

The sun bathes the hill in soft,
muted colors, a silent prayer.
The palpable darkness
beneath the ridge sketches
a flood of thought and feeling.

Perhaps this is why old men choose
to rise and greet the dawn.
To drink in memories of tears and joy
and beauty barely hinted at.

Morning Thoughts Over Coffee

I sit in silence on the small balcony
of our room with coffee, relaxed,
looking into the infinite pre-dawn
dark. Unseen in the blackness is
the Bahía de Banderas and the low,
plush range of the Sierra Madre.

Zig-zags of lightning flicker along
the mouth of the bay as warm moist air
from the ocean climbs the Sierra Madre.
The lightning illuminates the storms
as it blazes from cloud to cloud and
down into the water and mountains.

I feel the coolness of the breeze that
lifts the air up the mountains, smell
its tangy salt, taste it on my tongue,
see the mountains as day dawns,
hear the occasional growl of thunder
and the rhythmic boom of waves.

I think about that first morning of life
on our earth, billions of years ago.
Did it start something like this one?
A casual lightning strike creating life
in some shallow volcanic pond filled
with steamy, thick, primordial stew?

This morning's light discovers the tide
of life, lush green trees on mountains,
loose groups of frigate birds that soar
above the bay, lines of pelicans that
skim the tops of waves, and lovers
strolling hand in hand beside the surf.

Morning at the VLA Radio Telescope

Thick fog rolls up through Magdalena Gap
and spills out onto the high desert Plain
of San Agustin. The fog reaches beyond
the low buildings at the center's parking lot.
A light breeze stirs and the thick fog thins.

The tinker toy shape of a giant antenna,
a Cyclops, slowly appears. Soon another
and another until twenty-seven are there,
gathering faint radio signals from the dark
beyond the sun. Scientists watch and record
the birth and death of galaxies from millions
of light years ago.

Those scientists also listen for alien voices,
hoping to discover life on distant planets.
But if we hear them, will we understand
them any better than those we hear today
from our own planet?

Rock, Paper, Scissors

A game to settle disputes
or decide who gets that only
slice of pie or last beer.

A game kids play
just for fun or to decide
who goes first.

Rock breaks scissors –
scissors cut paper –
paper covers rock –

but water beats them all.
It washes away paper
and dissolves it over time.

Water soon rusts scissors,
turning blades into dust,
and as for rock …

Water slowly wears
rock away to create
the Grand Canyon,

the Rhine valley,
the Teton mountains,
isolated sea stacks …

Water nourishes and sustains
abundant life that takes joy
in its artful handiwork.

Song of Earth – song sung blue

> *A NASA spacecraft has recorded eerie-sounding radio emissions coming from our own planet. (NASA Science News)*

I have listened to these new recordings.
They are so clear. You do not hear static
or the ghostly whistling most recordings
from space have in common. They do not
seem in the slightest way eerie to my poet's
ear. Maybe they're eerie to the scientists
who did not expect to hear them.

But to me, they sound like our blue planet
singing a song similar to the recordings
of whales who sing to others to find them,
warn them, love them. Does our blue marble
sing love songs to the whales? Or does she sing
of pain because of man's brutality to her and
the creatures and flora that depend on her?

Is man the only creature who cannot hear
the song of the earth without electronics?
Will man hear earth's song and heed it, or
just sell recordings of a song sung blue?

Surprised by Joy

> Fair as a star, when only one
> Is shining in the sky

When I walk a path of flowering plum
or hyacinths, or pass a field
of blue-eyed grass or scarlet fireweed,
I smile and am glad.

But, when I'm hiking through the shade
of a mountain wood near a snow-fed creek
and find a solitary Calypso orchid,
my heart is overwhelmed by joy.

A single object of delight, demands
the eye enfold, examine, hold it fast.
And in that careful look my soul
rejoices in the varied hues of pink,
the slender stamen's gentle curve,
the tiny yellow specks
of pollen fluff.

High Plains Thunderstorm

He watches clouds build over the snowy
spine of mountains, becoming darker
as they grow. One thrusts up taller
than the rest and moves onto the plains,
dragging dark gray virga skirts,
stalking on legs of lightning.

He looks to the dry wheat and hopes the virga
becomes rain. His crops scorched by the sun
three summers now. He'll go bust if a storm
doesn't soon water his fields.

Sky turns green.
Meadowlarks stop singing.
Crows stop flying.
Grasses stop waving.
A great stillness.

The wind comes alive with a sudden gust
from the south, switching quickly west
and back again. Dust swirls from his fields,
hiding the storm until the wind takes it north,
and he can see the swirling darkness.

Shouting over the wind
to his wife, they race
to the root cellar,
close the heavy door.

They cling to each other,
listen to howl and clatter.
It lasts forever . . . and then
a more profound stillness.

They climb from the cellar. The barn roof
has smashed the house, milk house gone,
wheat, hail shredded. They hold each other
and cry.

Ridge Soaring in Virginia

This wind has travelled east
from my home in the Rockies
to join me in this glider as I
tack along this Virginia ridge.

I maintain altitude because
the wind slides up the ridge
and the warm rising air lifts
the wings of my light craft.

I turn back and forth across
the slope to watch two horses
gallop in the large rectangle
of their green pasture below.

I glance across the ridge and see
a golden eagle also soaring here.
He makes a steep turn to join me,
just feet away from my wing tip.

We spend the next hour soaring,
sharing each other's joy.

A Murder of Crows

A large, pompadoured crow
struts, stiff-legged, across the street,
breaking into quick crow hops
to gain the grass just ahead of
a speeding car. A slick-haired punk,
showing off for his peers — he's cool.

Two raucous, swirling groups
of screaming crows squabble and
threaten, claiming territory.
Rival gangs -- name-calling, posturing,
intimidating. They swarm as if to attack,
but veer off — a dangerous
West Side Story ballet.

Thousands of crows clutch winter-bare
limbs, creating black-leafed Gothic trees.
They settle into a ferocious silence.
Half an hour. No sound.
Then at an unseen, silent sign,
they explode out of the trees into
a frenzied, screeching mob — Choppers
and their leather-clad riders
roaring through Sturgis.

Do we fear large flocks of crows
because of Hitchcock's *The Birds*?
Or did the master of scare
use our innate fear?

After the Summer Solstice

The Sun, ever proud parent, wanting to display
the beauty of Earth, his treasured, spoiled child,
bathes it in his light. Earth thrives in the warmth

of his light, bearing flowers, fruit, nurturing
new-born creatures. He wants man to revel
in that plentitude, so each day the light hides

his other children, the planets, Venus, Mars,
Jupiter, Saturn, Earth's Moon, the starry river
of the Milky Way, Orion, and Scorpio's red eye,

the nightly shuffle of the Great Bear, the glorious
infinity of the galaxy-filled Universe. And Earth,
fickle child, soon tires of light and slowly leans
into winter's darkness and magnificent night sky.

Ode to a Fairy Primrose

You stand there, not three inches tall,
on a delicate carpet of pale green tundra,
just around a windy corner from a cirque,

a sheer thousand-foot granite cliff, carved
there slowly by a glacier twenty thousand
years ago. The summer morning shadow

of Longs Peak, three thousand feet above,
lifts from you each morning. Your five frail
pink petals belie your toughness. You were

buried under yards of snow this winter,
seared by temperatures well below zero
most of the year, and the soil just feet

beneath your roots is frozen even now.
Nine of you stand in a cluster yards away
from other blooms. This is God's garden,

and there is plenty of room, if not time,
to grow, but you stay small, using your
strength, not for size, but for beauty.

To See a World in a Grain of Sand

A small dark hole at the edge of space
no bigger than a grain of sand held out
at arms length. Curious scientists point

the Hubble telescope and let it watch
that dark for ten days, then for eleven.
It searches thirteen billion light years out

and finds that the darkness, that grain
of sand, holds three thousand galaxies,
each with hundreds of billions of stars

like our Milky Way. The human mind
cannot begin to grasp the magnitude
of that discovery. How then to grasp

the wonder of the God who flung
those galaxies and stars for us to find?

Sunspots Explained

A Villanelle of War

The mortal soul is shattered by a war
much like a body blown by bomb or shot,
the pain recedes but never goes away.

The guilt remains because he could not save
those men who died when he arrived too late,
his mortal soul was shattered by the war.

His terror as the bullets passed his plane,
and snapped at him as if the jaws of death,
the fear recedes but never goes away.

He often thinks of enemies he killed,
their mothers, wives, and children left to grieve,
their souls forever shattered by the war.

How can he ever clear that guilt or ask
forgiveness from the men whose lives he took?
The guilt recedes but never goes away.

He sees friends' bodies strewn in rice-green fields,
and ghosts of men he killed in burning woods.
His mortal soul is shattered by that war.
The pain recedes but never goes away.

Sunspots Explained

> ... *researchers announced that a jet stream
> deep inside the sun is migrating slower
> than usual through the star's interior,
> giving rise to the current lack of sunspots.
> (NASA Science News)*

Scientists using telescopes
and pressure instruments
and the new study
of helioseismology
have mapped the sun's
subterranean jet stream
and discovered why sunspots,
violent events on the sun's surface,
have lessened.

Might we turn
those instruments earthward
to create helioseismic maps
of subterranean jet streams
that cause earth spots, violent
events on the earth's surface?

Those jet streams
could have triggered
Wounded Knee, Antietam,
Gettysburg, and Sand Creek.
Helioseismic maps
certainly would explain
Dachau, Dresden, Nanking
Hiroshima and Nagasaki.

Had we known sooner,
we might have reduced
the suffering in Bosnia,
Palestine, Darfur, and
the World Trade Center.

Hiroshima, August 6, 1945, 8:15 AM

Yoshiko Yamamoto looks up from her book
where she sits on a bench in the school yard
and sees an American bomber cross the blue
sky over the city and turn abruptly around.
It's so high she cannot hear it. She looks back
at her book. Suddenly the morning stillness
erupts in the light and heat of a hundred suns,
followed by a sound as if the very universe
were being shredded.

                    She hears her own screams,
those of others around her, the crackle of fire.
As she slides into unconsciousness, she senses,
more than feels, her hair burn, her face melt,
her lungs scorch. Then, silence.

Akio Suzuki, 13, sits on a rock in a small valley
several miles from the city. He eats wild grapes
he picked from bushes by the road as he rests
from the work his school assigned him for his
semester break. Suddenly he is blinded by light
far brighter than the sun, his ears assaulted
by a thunder that shakes the hills and pounds
his chest. He shuts his eyes, covers his ears,
and screams his terror.

                    Finally, the thunder stops
and he opens his eyes. He sees a huge column
of smoke race into the blue sky, hears the terrible
thunder echoing through the hills. He cries out
for his mother and sister in the city over the hills.
Sobs shake his body. Then, silence.

October 24, 1962, 3:45 AM

We're headed west at forty thousand feet
above the blackness of Atlantic cold.
A tiny light on the ocean miles below
marks a freighter bound for who knows where,
and blinking red and green lights just ahead
come from another tanker just like us.
An hour ago, we each were pumping fuel
into an eight-jet bomber with a crew
of six and bellies crammed with atom bombs.

While thousands of miles away, directly south,
a fleet of Russian boats draws near a line
of US warships who have quarantined
Cuba's ports. If the ships don't turn around,
the bombers we refueled will fly on east,
descend, and level Russian cities with
their bombs. And as their bombs explode,
Soviet missiles will land on bases we
are headed for, and vaporize them, with
our loved ones, in a sun-bright flash of light.

We cruise along this quiet night, maintain
our altitude, our thoughts, unspoken fears,
and pray the light we see this coming dawn
will be the peaceful sunrise in the east.

A Glacial Erratic

The large granite boulder has rested
here in the oak and pitch pine forest
for thousands of years. Its top is broad
and flat with patches of yellow lichen.

Twenty thousand years earlier the
Wisconsin Glacier pried the boulder
out of continental bedrock, pushing it
and rolling it until it sat on this hill.

Four children and their gray-haired
guide sit on it in the warm sunshine,
eating jelly sandwiches. They listen
to delightful tales the woman tells.

They play in the sunshine and scramble
on its cracked and pitted gray sides.
This is not their first time at the rock.
Their pied piper, their grandmother,

brings them here often, leading them
on the long, raucous, and joyous trek.
The kids don't know about the glacier
and it would mean nothing to them.

The kids also don't know that one of them
will be ravaged and scarred by a jungle war
and his memories of these sun-filled days
will help him recover from his despair.

He will remember his grandmother's laugh and those walks to the ancient rock and find that the gentle power of her love, like the slow power of the glacier, will conquer his fears.

Darkness at the Bottom of the Fog

He drives through hoar frost coated
on trees by a dense fog. As he passes
a small pond, a flock of geese drops
out of the fog to splash into it.

He lowers through fog toward the sea,
searching for the bottom, descending
at 500 feet per minute, slowing the descent
gradually as he approaches one hundred feet.
A shadow of darkness appears. The darkness
grows, until at fifty feet it overwhelms the gray.
His fear overcomes insanity, and he shoves
the throttle, and climbs through the fog
to the bright blue morning sky.

The geese know the darkness in their descent
is the pond, a place of safety for them.
His had been a descent into a darkness
gradually grown there by months of combat,
killing men who tried to kill him. He wanted
never to face that darkness again.

The Sudden End of the Firefight

The jet races low over the fields toward the tree line
where a small cloud of white smoke rises
from a marking rocket. As the jet nears the smoke,
six shiny cans of napalm tumble from it,
two by two by two,
exploding into a rolling ball of fire
that engulfs the trees.

When the burning slows, troops move forward
to rout the enemy who has wounded
and killed their comrades.
They find only death from the fire.
Forty-five enemy killed.
There is ecstasy over the victory.

In the decades since, in nightmares,
daymares, memories, that jet races
again and again and again
to the trees and releases its napalm,
two by two by two.
But now there is no ecstasy,
only sadness and grief and guilt.

I Will Fight No More Forever

He cries quietly at the black granite wall,
touching the names of young friends
who did not come home with him.

He steps back and is startled to see
his own sad eyes, weathered face
staring out from among etched names.

He sorts through scattered thoughts
of battles in a place he did not want
to be, fighting a people he did not hate.

He surrenders to words of Chief Joseph,
Nez Perce tribe surrounded, defeated,
saying, "I will fight no more forever."

The Old Picture in the Back Hall

I walk into the back hall, stop, bend down
to take the leash off the dog, catch my breath
after our three mile walk. I glance at a picture
hanging to my right. A young man smiles back
at me, leans jauntily against a small, gray airplane,
right hand resting easily on a pistol at his hip.
The plane is in a revetment built from rusty
fifty-five gallon drums, and in the background
puffy clouds hang in a pale Vietnamese sky.

The picture, taken forty-four years ago — its color
faded from sunlight and age — has hung in that spot
for a dozen years. I walk past it several times a day,
without noticing it. But today, the stark realization
of the passing of all that time catches me up.

What that young man did then, I could no longer do,
or even want to do. His deeds were adventurous
and exciting to him. Today they are the fearsome
and haunting memories of an old warrior.

War Memorial at Holy Ghost Church

His head awkwardly bent, his boots awry,
the tarp that cloaks his body hides his form.
It also hides his face so we can't see
his dying pain or blissful letting go.

His helmet rests beside his blast bent legs
and boots which jut beyond the marble base.
So many busy people walking past
do not look up and see him lying there.

There where the Holy Ghost has lifted him
toward the heaven his sacrifice has earned.
They also do not see his arm, the only
piece of him not hidden by the cloth.

He reaches out and down as if to grasp
my hand to have me pull him back to life.

The Church Ruins at Quang Ngai

I see it each morning just south of the river
as I climb to the west to begin my day.
I can look into the church, its roof and west
wall gone, the others damaged. The gothic
windows long have lost their colored glass;
only spidery frames remain. The church
is empty of furniture and debris as if that
has more value than the church. No one I ask
has any idea when the church was destroyed
or why it has never been rebuilt.

It must have been built by French Catholics
before the French were kicked out of Vietnam.
Perhaps the people didn't want to remember
French arrogance or that of the church, so they
never rebuilt that monument to them. Perhaps,
with the horror of many years of war swirling
around their lives, the church became irrelevant.

And so it stands, abandoned. Sampans float
slowly past in the muddy river a hundred yards
from the back wall, farmers shoulder heavy
loads or drive donkey carts on the dirt road
past the front door. The cemetery lays beyond
the destroyed wall, and rice paddies sit green
to the east. That church seems a monument
also to our own foolish arrogance.

Descending into Puerto Vallarta

We drop through layers of clouds,
slipping in and out of bright sunlight.
Finally Mexico comes into sight
through the ragged cloud bottoms.
Rain soaked hills and mountains rise,
covered with dense jungle,
dotted with white veils of mist.

> Forty year old memories and fears
> rise as he descends into a jungle valley
> west of Khe Sanh after a monsoon rain.
> He fears that guns below track his plane.
> He fears the chaos about to swallow him.

I shake my head to clear it and
force myself to look at cars driving
through lush valleys, plush resorts,
the beach, my wife next to me.
We descend into Puerto Vallarta.

Book of Names

In a book of names thick as my fist, I look
for names of friends so I can find them etched
into the mirror of the polished granite wall.

Simmons, killed directing artillery on a VC force
that ambushed comrades in a snarl of green jungle.
I see his impish, farm boy, face smile out at me
from a Texas sky blue morning where we learned to fly.

Johnson, the Jersey speedster, 100 yard record holder.
We lived in facing rooms at the end of the hall in basic.
He was fast, but not fast enough to outrun bullets from
an enemy gun, shot down on a starless Laotian night.

I walk deeper into the wall — It's above my head now,
etched with more names as the war crescendos.

Stone, who I woke one Asian dawn to rescue
ambushed troops. Shot down in a rice paddy.
I sorted through his clothes, letters, books,
and sent them home to his wife and kids.

Meadows, shot down up north, missing, a cross etched
beside his name. Three years we shared a squadron.
Gentle friend, groomsman at my wedding, life cut short.
His wife so grieved she took her life.

I start back to the fist-sized book to look for names,
but tears stop me.

My Band of Brothers

We few, we happy few ...

I meet them in the grocery store
parking lot or the hardware store.
I recognize them by a license plate,
a window decal, a bumper sticker,
the baseball caps they're wearing.

We stop briefly to chat, sharing
where we served, Quang Ngai,
Can Tho, Cu Chi, An Khe, Saigon.
We were there at different times
and had very different duties, but
we share a bond, we served our
country and we are brothers.

It was an unpopular war in which
those called to duty came home to be
spit upon, called vile names, shunned
in polite society, never welcomed, made
to suffer in silence and all alone.

So today when we meet, and mention
those days, backs straighten, eyes take on
a look of pride, and we remember those
we fought with, those who did not return.
A nod and on our way, but not without
saying, "Welcome home, Brother."

About the Author

Art Elser is a poet and writer who has been published in many journals and anthologies. His latest book, *As The Crow Flies*, is a collection of 120 haiku selected from over 2,000 he has written. His other books include a memoir, *What's It All About, Alfie?*, and three books of poetry, *We Leave the Safety of the Sea*, *A Death at Tollgate Creek,* and *As The Crow Flies*. Art lives in Denver with his wife, Kathy, and their pup, Walker.

www.ingramcontent.com/pod-product-compliance
Lightning Source LLC
Chambersburg PA
CBHW021135300426
44113CB00006B/443